OXFORDSHI...
Woodeaton Manor
Woodeaton
Oxford OX3 9TS
Telephone: Oxford 58722

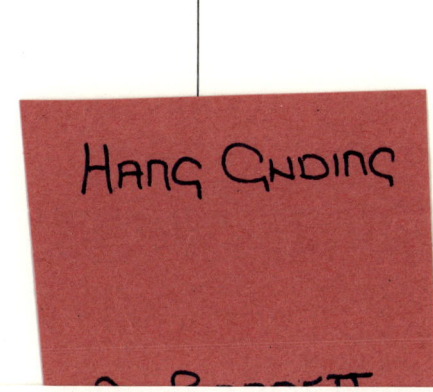

Hang Gliding

JS 797.55   BARRETT, N.
               Hang gliding

**OXFORDSHIRE COUNTY LIBRARIES
SCHOOLS LIBRARY SERVICE**

PICTURE LIBRARY
HANG GLIDING

Norman Barrett

Franklin Watts

London   New York   Sydney   Toronto

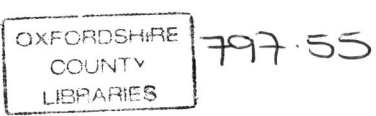

© 1987 Franklin Watts

First published in Great Britain 1987 by
Franklin Watts
12a Golden Square
London W1R 4BA

First published in the USA by
Franklin Watts Inc
387 Park Avenue South
New York
N.Y. 10016

First published in Australia by
Franklin Watts
14 Mars Road
Lane Cove
2066 NSW

UK ISBN: 0 86313 513 7
US ISBN: 0-531-10 350-1
Library of Congress Catalog Card
Number 86-51223

Printed in Italy

Designed by
Barrett & Willard

Photographs by
All-Sport
All-Sport/Vandystadt
N.S. Barrett Collection
Eric Raymond

Illustration by
Rhoda & Robert Burns

Technical Consultant
David Worth

Contents

Introduction	6
The hang glider	8
Taking off and landing	10
Flying	12
Cross-country	18
Mountain flying	20
Competition flying	22
Assisted flight	24
The story of hang gliding	28
Facts and records	30
Glossary	31
Index	32

Introduction

△ Soaring through the air with just a light framework and a pair of wings for support is the nearest that people can get to flying like birds.

Soaring high above the ground in a hang glider, people can enjoy the thrills of flying like a bird. Hang gliding is a new sport, exciting to perform and beautiful to watch.

It can also be dangerous if strict safety precautions are not taken. Hang gliders do not have engines, but in other respects they fly like any other heavier-than-air craft.

Most people do hang gliding for the sheer enjoyment of the sport. But there is also some competition, including racing.

Hang gliders can now stay aloft for hours on end. Cross-country and mountain flying have become popular.

Powered hang gliding is also a growing sport. The machines, which use small engines, are called microlights.

△ Hang gliders built to support two flyers may be used for instructing novices. This one has a sitting harness.

The hang glider

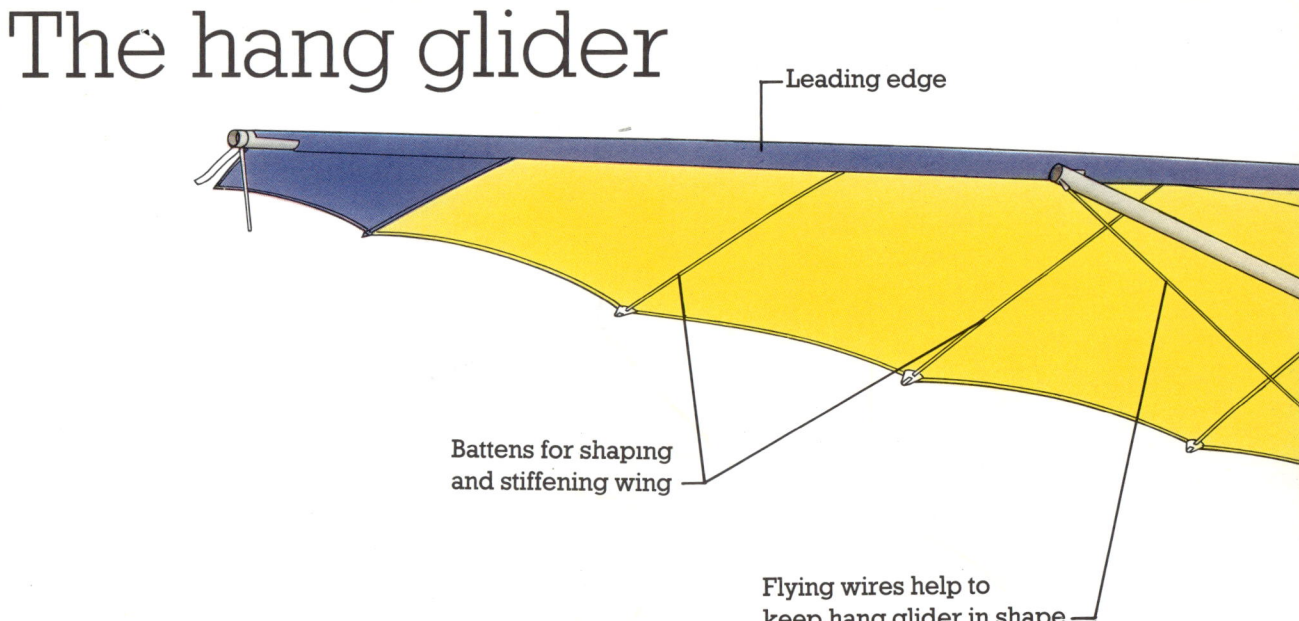

Airflow
Air travels faster over the curved top surface of a wing than the flatter bottom surface. This means that the pressure is lower at the top, creating lift.

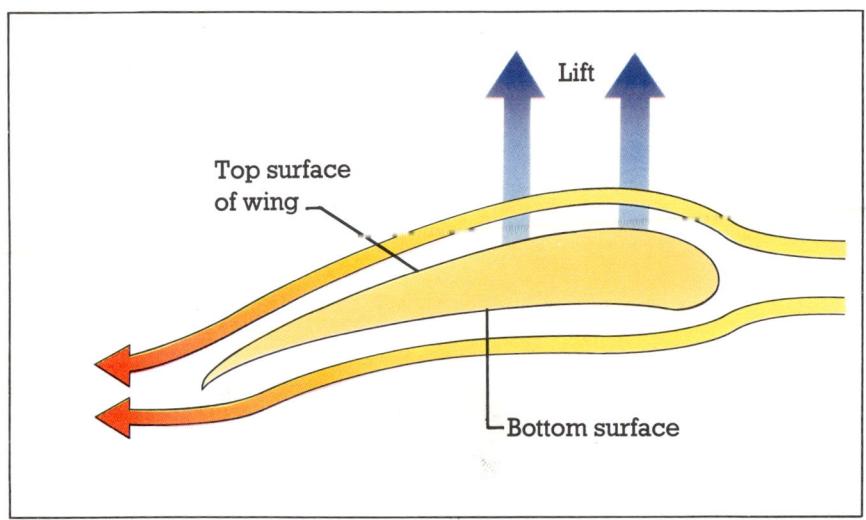

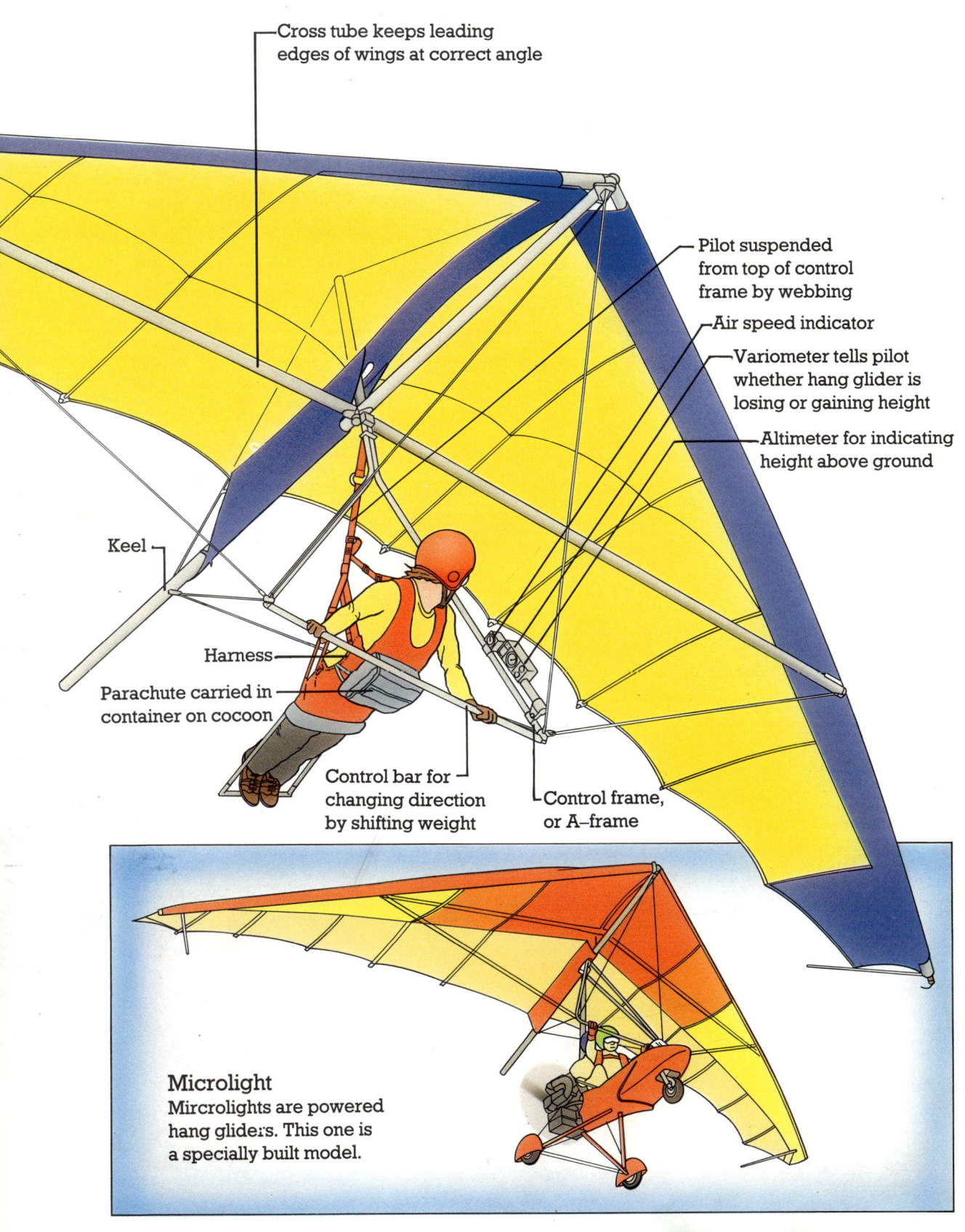

Microlight
Microlights are powered hang gliders. This one is a specially built model.

Taking off and landing

Hang gliders get airborne by running off a hill or a cliff into the wind. A clear run of about 10 m (10 yd) may be needed to get up sufficient speed for take-off. The nose of the hang glider must be raised at the correct angle, called the "angle of attack".

Landing must be into the wind. The pilot slows down by moving his or her weight back, which raises the nose. The aim is to drop gently to the ground with both feet.

△ Preparing for take-off at the top of a hill. Only a short run is needed, depending on the wind speed. In a wind of over about 20 km/h (12 mph) no run is needed at all. In winds over about 32 km/h (20 mph) the glider has to be held down by a "wire man" on the front flying wires.

△ As the airflow over the wing increases, the sail is filled and lifts the pilot off the ground. The pilot moves his weight forward to gain air speed by pulling in on the control bar.

◁ Coming in to land, the pilot drops out of the harness and holds the uprights of the control frame ready to push out just before the feet touch the ground.

Flying

Flying a hang glider is similar to flying any other aircraft. A certain air speed must be kept up to prevent it stalling, or losing lift. This is low for a hang glider, only about 24–32 km/h (15–20 mph).

The simplest hang gliders are controlled by the pilot shifting weight. To increase speed and dive, the weight is shifted forward. To slow down, it is shifted back. To turn to left or right, the weight is moved in that direction.

△ The hang glider pilot uses the control bar to shift weight and control the speed and direction of flight.

▷ Hang glider pilots look for rising air currents to enable them to soar. These are most easily found at hills or ridges, where the air is deflected upwards.

◁ Dual flying is a good way to learn how to hang glide. The instructor can demonstrate the controls and allow the learner to take over and perform various movements. Dual flying also allows the learner to get used to the feeling of flying without having to worry about what to do.

Dual flying is also useful for beginners tackling new hills. Each hill has its own system of air currents and these always take a little getting used to.

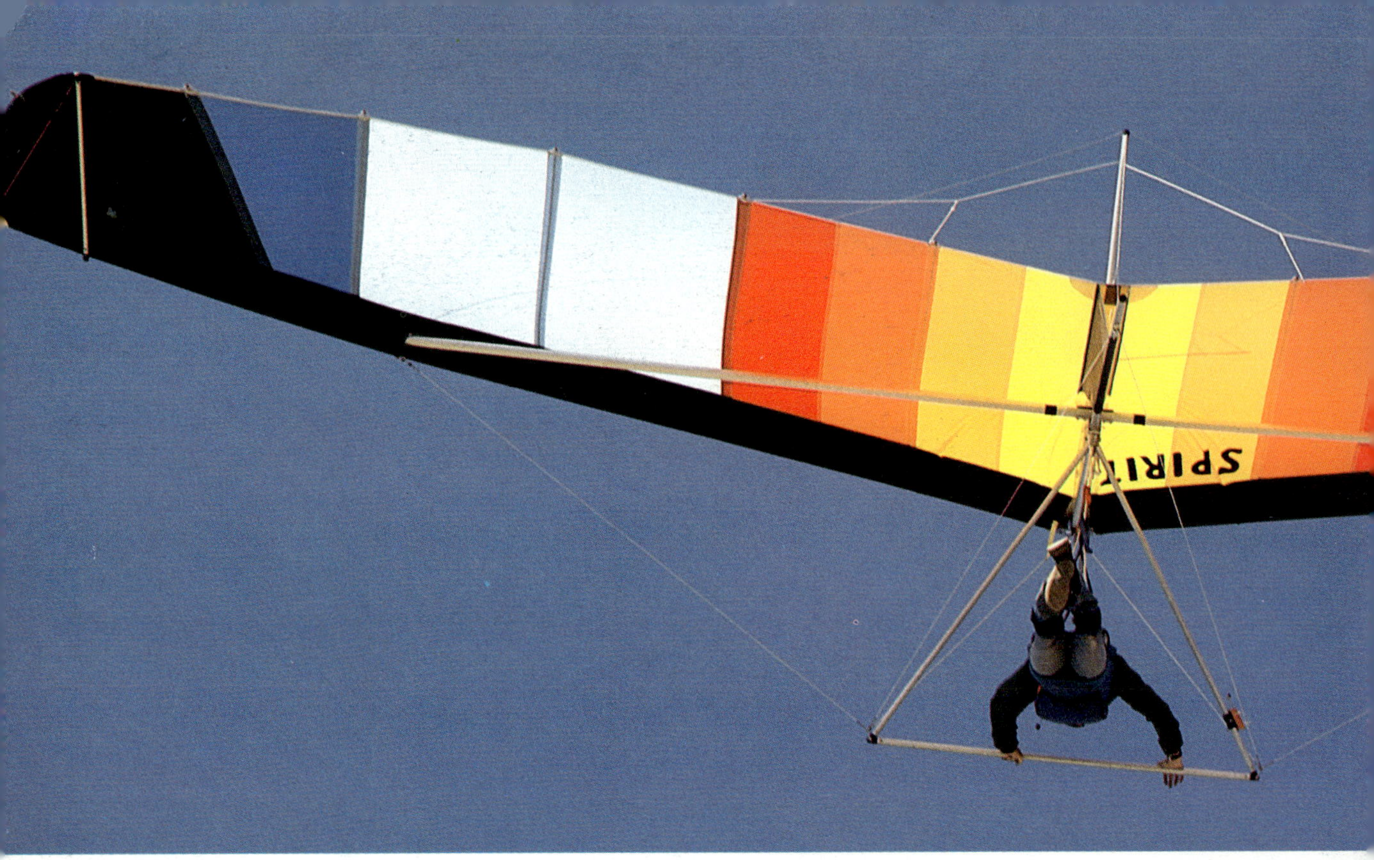

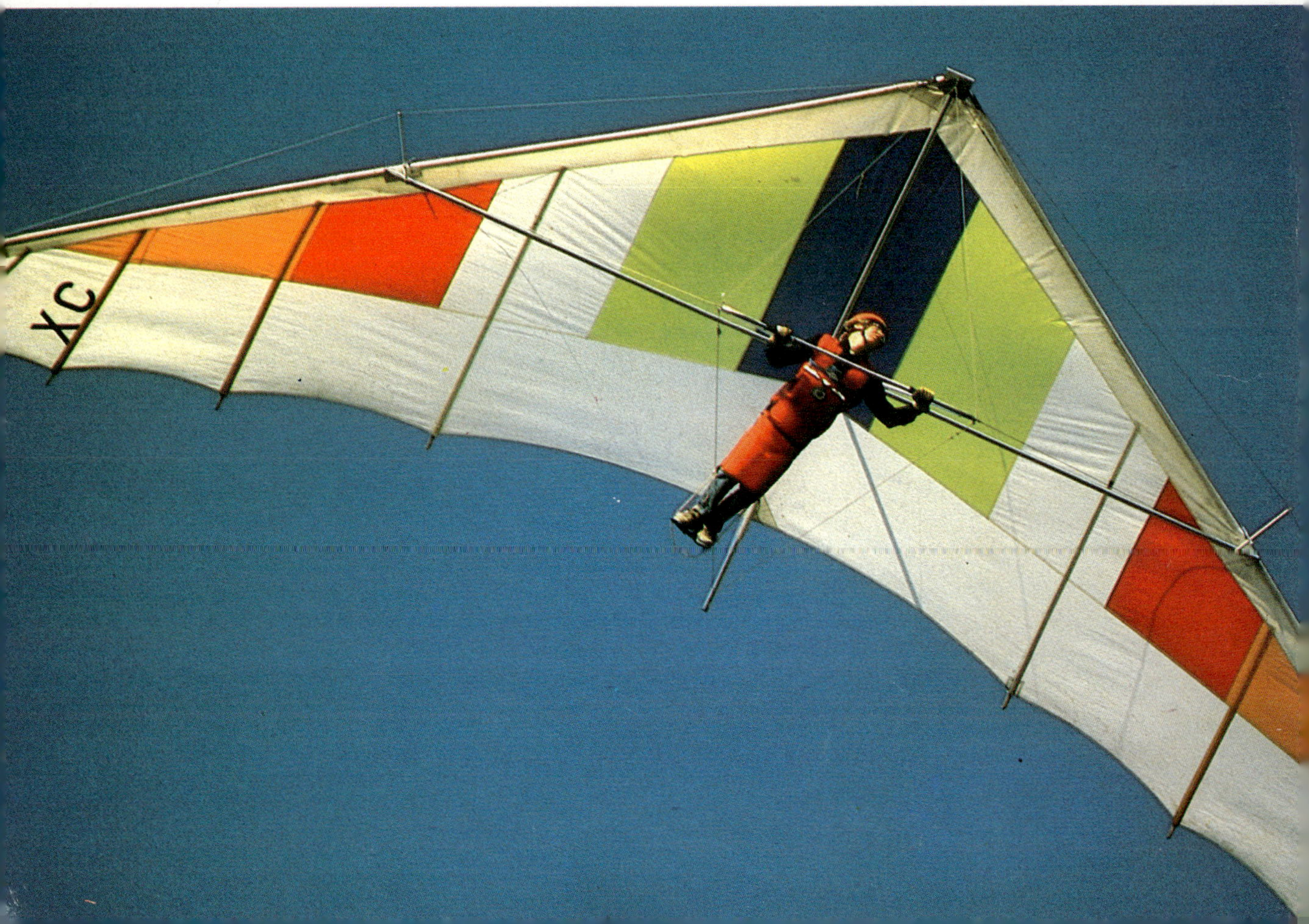
XC

Hang gliders are made in various shapes and designs, some for speed, others for ease of flying. They are colourful against the blue sky and graceful to watch as they soar through the air.

Cross-country

Experienced hang glider pilots enjoy flying long distances over the countryside. They must be able to find favourable air currents, called thermals. These are huge "bubbles" of rising warm air.

As the ground becomes warm, it heats the air above it, and this rises. Thermals depend on the type of ground, the weather and the time of day. An expert learns to read the signs.

▽ As a hang glider leaves the familiar ridge or hill, the pilot must rely on rising air currents to stay aloft.

Flat fields and low-lying villages warm up quickly, whereas wooded areas warm up more slowly. But forests retain their heat until late in the day. These are the kinds of signs cross-country fliers note when they are looking for thermals.

In addition to the wonderful feeling of flying, cross-country hang gliders can enjoy the beautiful scenery below them.

19

Mountain flying

△ Flying in the thin air above the mountains, the pilot is enclosed in a special cocoon harness for warmth as well as for extra speed. The streamlined shape offers less air resistance. Modern equipment and materials enable hang gliders to make long flights over mountains.

◁ A view from below as a hang glider takes off from a mountain ramp.

Some of the most spectacular hang gliding can be enjoyed high up in the mountains. But it is not like ridge flying. The air behaves very differently in the mountains and it is much harder to read the signs.

A specially built ramp may be needed for launching, because the mountain air is thin and a faster take-off speed is required. Launching from a clifftop may be tricky because of the wind patterns.

Competition flying

There are various types of competition for hang gliders.

Ridge races are there-and-back flights between points on a suitable ridge. In cross-country racing, competitors may have to fly to several points long distances apart.

There are also events for the greatest straight-line distance flown from the launch. In a pylon task, the competitors have to fly round specially marked points.

▷ A competitor prepares for take-off. He holds the harness in his left hand to avoid tripping over it as he runs. His parachute is carried in front, and various instruments are attached to the control frame.

▽ Crowds gather to watch an international hang gliding contest. Ski resorts in summer provide good facilities for both competitors and spectators.

Assisted flight

Suitable hills are not always available for launching hang gliders and sometimes the conditions are not right. Other methods, such as launching from a balloon or towing, are not as satisfactory.

Powered flight, however, is becoming popular. Hang gliders with small engines attached are called microlights. Some microlights are specially built.

▷ A hang glider suspended from the basket of a hot-air balloon and about to be launched. This has proved to be a difficult exercise and is usually reserved for exhibitions.

▽ Enjoying a microlight flight in the setting sun. The engine can be clearly seen in front of the wings.

▷ With the pilot in a comfortable sitting position, modern microlight flying looks like the early days of aeroplanes. The many flying wires to be seen help to strengthen the craft.

Microlights may be operated by ailerons – moving flaps on the wings – instead of by shifting weight.

The story of hang gliding

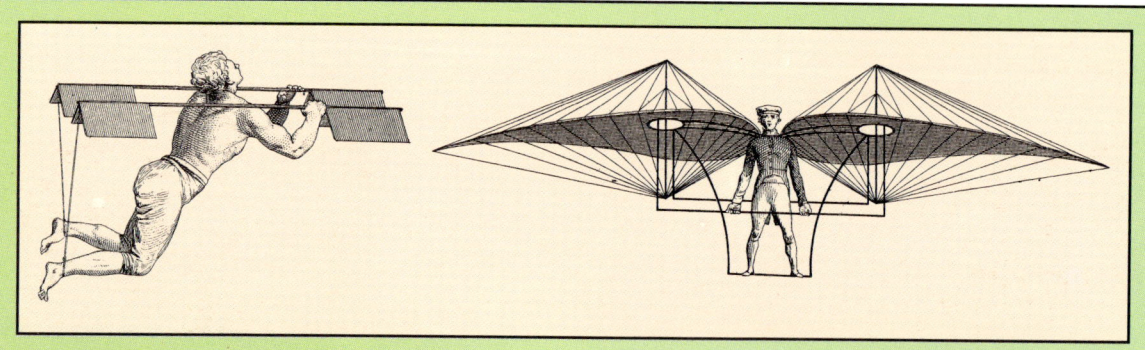

△ Two early attempts at flying. The curious apparatus on the left was devised by a French locksmith called Le Besnier in the 1670s, and had to be worked by hands and feet. His claims to have made short flights with it were never recognized.

The device on the right was invented by Swiss clockmaker Jacob Degen in 1806. He demonstrated it in Paris, adding a balloon to make it rise. But when he kept blowing away, the crowd lost their patience and broke up the apparatus.

Fly like a bird

People have always dreamed of being able to fly like birds. Through the ages people have invented all kinds of devices to enable them to flap "wings" like birds. But human muscles are not powerful enough in relation to their body weight to make this happen. This was known in the late 1600s, but people still kept trying to fly.

Birdmen

People who tried to fly were always regarded as somewhat odd. These so-called birdmen would jump off cliffs, bridges or towers with only their homemade wings made of canvas, linen or silk. These attempts mostly had disastrous results.

Pioneers of hang gliding

The man regarded as the "father" of hang gliding is the German pioneer Otto Lilienthal. In the late 1800s, he made more than 2,000 short "glides" from hills in fixed-wing hang gliders. Eventually, in 1896, he crashed from a height of 30 m (100 ft) and was killed.

Inspired by Lilienthal, the British inventor Percy Pilcher experimented with both powerless and powered machines, but he, too, was killed in 1899.

The birth of modern hang gliding

With the invention of powered flight by the Wright brothers in 1903, hang gliding took a back seat for over 50 years, although gliding in sailplanes was developed.

It was not until the 1960s that the idea of the hang glider was reborn, and it happened in California. A sailwing design of NASA scientist Dr Francis Rogallo for carrying space instruments was adapted by some students for skimming flights over the ground. At the same time, some Australian water-skiers began experimenting with man-carrying kites behind their boats. When the swing seat they used was fitted to a Rogallo wing, the first practical hang glider had arrived.

△ Hang gliding in 1896 – the British pioneer Percy Pilcher in his "Hawk".

No limits

The first hang gliders could do no more than glide down from a hill for a few hundred metres. As the sport developed, experts began to stay aloft for long periods and travel several kilometres. Now, with the great advances in design and techniques, there seems to be no limit to the duration and distance of flights.

△ Otto Lilienthal glides down from his home-made hill in 1895.

△ Hang gliders can now stay aloft for long periods.

29

Facts and records

△ World champion John Pendry in an Airwave Magic 4 hang glider.

Greatest distance

The British hang glider pilot John Pendry has dominated competitive hang gliding in the mid-1980s, winning the world championship in 1985. In 1983, flying an Airwave Magic 3 from California to Nevada in the United States, he set the official world distance record of 300.6 km (186.8 miles).

At the same place and on the same day, another British pilot, Judy Leden, set the women's distance record of 233.9 km (145.3 miles).

Going up

The record for the greatest gain of height was set in California by a US pilot, Larry Tudor, in 1985. He reached a height of 4,343.4 m (14,150 ft) from his take-off spot.

Glossary

Angle of attack
The angle at which the surface of the wing meets the airflow.

Battens
Rods of fibreglass or a similar material, placed in sleeves in the wing to stiffen it and give it shape.

Cocoon
A streamlined "suit" encasing the pilot, used for speed and for warmth at high altitudes.

Control bar
The bar at the bottom of the triangular control frame suspended from the wings. The pilot holds the control bar, shifting his or her weight around to change direction.

Flying wires
Wires connecting the control frame and other parts of the hang glider to maintain the correct shape and to strengthen the structure.

Keel
Tube running between the two parts of the wing from nose to tail.

Microlight
A type of hang glider powered by a small engine.

Pylon task
A form of competition in which the pilots have to round a number of points called pylons. These are not real pylons, and the pilots are often asked to photograph the turning points as evidence of having rounded them.

Ramp
A sloping take-off area built to help take-off from difficult places.

Ridge
A long, even hill, ideal for hang gliding because of the regular upcurrent of air flowing up and over its top surface.

Rogallo wing
The triangular-shaped hang glider, named after Dr Francis Rogallo whose work led to the modern craft.

Stall
Loss of smooth airflow over the wings, resulting in a sudden loss of lift. Beginners are taught how to go into a stall so that they can learn how to correct it.

Thermal
A rising current of warm air, sought by hang glider pilots and used for gaining height.

Index

A-frame 9
aileron 26
air current 15, 18
airflow 8
air speed indicator 9
altimeter 9
angle of attack 10, 31

balloon 24, 25
batten 8, 31
birdmen 28

cocoon 21, 31
competition flying 22, 23
control bar 9, 11, 12, 31
control frame 9, 11
cross-country 7, 18, 19, 22

distance record 30
dual flying 15

engine 24

fixed-wing hang glider 28
flying wire 9, 10, 26, 31

gliding 29

harness 7, 9, 11, 22
height record 30

keel 9, 31
kite 29

landing 10
leading edge 8, 9

launching 21, 24
Leden, Judy 30
lift 8
Lilienthal, Otto 28, 29

microlight 7, 9, 24, 26, 31
mountain flying 7, 20, 21

parachute 9, 22
Pendry, John 30
Pilcher, Percy 28, 29
pilot 9, 10, 18, 26
pylon task 22, 31

racing 7
ramp 20, 21, 31
ridge 13, 18, 21, 31
ridge race 22
Rogallo, Francis 29
Rogallo wing 31

sailwing 29
stall 12, 31

take-off 10, 30
take-off speed 21
thermal 18, 31
towing 24
Tudor, Larry 30

variometer 9

wing 8
wire man 10
world championships 30
Wright brothers 29